MARCH ON WASHINGTON

Robin Johnson

Crabtree Publishing Company

www.crabtreebooks.com

Crabtree Publishing Company

www.crabtreebooks.com

Author: Robin Johnson
Publishing plan research and development:
Sean Charlebois, Reagan Miller
Crabtree Publishing Company
Photo research: Robin Johnson
Editors: Rachel Minay, Kathy Middleton
Proofreader: Crystal Sikkens
Design: Clare Nicholas/Tim Mayer
(Mayer Media)
Cover design: Ken Wright
**Production coordinator and prepress
technician:** Ken Wright
Print coordinator: Katherine Berti

Produced for Crabtree Publishing by
White-Thomson Publishing

Photographs:
Alamy: Everett Collection Historical: pp. 18–19; **Associated Press:** front cover; **Corbis:** pp. 22–23, 24–25; Bettmann: pp. 6–7, 28–29, 33, 36–37; Jack Moebes: pp. 10–11; Wally McNamee: pp. 38, 44–45; **Getty Images:** pp. 8–9, 30–31, 34–35, 42–43; NBCU Photo Bank: pp. 40–41; Time & Life Pictures: pp. 12–13, 20–21; **Library of Congress:** Carl Van Vechten: p. 27, Orlando Fernandez: pp. 16, 17; Warren K. Leffler: pp. 1, 3, 4–5, 14–15; **Press Association:** AP/Press Association Images: pp. 26, 32, 39; **White-Thomson Publishing/Stefan Chabluk:** p. 23.

Library and Archives Canada Cataloguing in Publication

Johnson, Robin (Robin R.)
March on Washington / Robin Johnson.

(Crabtree chrome)
Includes index.
Issued also in electronic formats.
ISBN 978-0-7787-1101-8 (bound).--ISBN 978-0-7787-1121-6 (pbk.)

1. March on Washington for Jobs and Freedom (1963 : Washington, D.C.)--Juvenile literature. 2. Civil rights demonstrations--Washington (D.C.)--History--20th century--Juvenile literature. 3. African Americans--Civil rights--Juvenile literature. I. Title. II. Series: Crabtree chrome

F200.J65 2013   j323.1196073'09046   C2012-908188-4

Library of Congress Cataloging-in-Publication Data

Johnson, Robin (Robin R.)
March on Washington / Robin Johnson.
pages cm. -- (Crabtree chrome)
Includes index.
ISBN 978-0-7787-1101-8 (reinforced library binding : alk. paper) -- ISBN 978-0-7787-1121-6 (pbk. : alk. paper) -- ISBN 978-1-4271-9243-1 (electronic pdf) -- ISBN 978-1-4271-9167-0 (electronic html)
1. March on Washington for Jobs and Freedom (1963 : Washington, D.C.)--Juvenile literature. 2. Civil rights demonstrations--Washington (D.C.)--History--20th century--Juvenile literature. 3. African Americans--Civil rights--History--20th century--Juvenile literature. I. Title.

F200.J64 2013
323.1196'073--dc23
2012047917

Crabtree Publishing Company

www.crabtreebooks.com   1-800-387-7650
Printed in Canada/012013/MA20121217

Published in Canada
Crabtree Publishing
616 Welland Ave.
St. Catharines, ON
L2M 5V6

Published in the United States
Crabtree Publishing
PMB 59051
350 Fifth Avenue, 59th Floor
New York, New York 10118

Published in the United Kingdom
Crabtree Publishing
Maritime House
Basin Road North, Hove
BN41 1WR

Published in Australia
Crabtree Publishing
3 Charles Street
Coburg North
VIC 3058

Contents

Black and White

EM
EQUALS
FREEDOM

WE DEMAND EQUAL RIGHTS NOW!

WE MARCH

Changing Times

The 1950s and 1960s were a time of great change in the United States. Many people questioned the rules and laws of the country. They fought for the freedom to do and say what they wanted.

▶ *In the 1960s, African Americans had to fight for equal rights in jobs, voting, education, healthcare, and housing.*

Civil Rights

Black Americans did not have the same rights as white Americans at the time. They could not vote, work, learn, or live as they pleased. African Americans fought hard for their **civil rights**.

> "Every American ought to have the right to be treated as he would wish to be treated ... But this is not the case."
>
> U.S. President John F. Kennedy, in office 1961–63

civil rights: the rights given to people by their government

Separate Ways

In the South, laws kept African Americans from going to the same schools, hospitals, or parks as white people. They had to shop in different stores and eat at different restaurants. They used separate restrooms, water fountains, and phone booths.

FOR COLORED ONLY

Northern States

Segregation was not as common in the northern states as it was in the South. But black people in the North still did not have all the rights that white people had. It was much harder for African Americans to get the jobs or homes they wanted.

▼ *In the 1950s and 1960s, African Americans were called "colored" people or "Negroes."*

segregation: the separation of one group of people from another

Fighting for Their Rights

Taking Action

African Americans tried to change the laws of the United States. Some people went to court to fight segregation in schools, motels, and other public places. Other people took their **protests** to the streets.

Rosa Parks

In 1955, in Montgomery, Alabama, a black woman named Rosa Parks took a stand—by sitting down. Parks boldly refused to give her seat on a bus to a white passenger. She was arrested and became a hero for civil rights.

◀ *Rosa Parks was called "the first lady of civil rights."*

"We were human beings and we should be treated as such."

Rosa Parks

protests: actions to show that people disagree with something

Peaceful Protests

Many African Americans took part in peaceful protests to show they wanted the laws changed. In some towns and cities, black students sat in whites-only restaurants and politely asked to be served. Others visited whites-only beaches, libraries, theaters, and other public places they were not allowed to go.

Bus Stop

African Americans also fought back by refusing to buy or do certain things. After Rosa Parks was arrested, thousands of black people refused to ride the city buses. The bus company lost a lot of money. The **boycott** lasted for more than a year, until segregation on Montgomery buses was finally stopped.

NATIONAL HEADQUARTERS
MARCH
ON
WASHINGTON
FOR JOBS
& FREEDOM
WED. AUG. 28

The peaceful protests of African Americans sometimes turned ugly. White people in the South sprayed protesters with powerful fire hoses. They set fire to the homes of black people and to buses carrying them. Many black people were arrested. They were attacked, beaten, and even killed.

◀ *This picture shows students taking part in a "sit-in" protest at a whites-only lunch counter in Greensboro, North Carolina.*

boycott: a refusal to buy or use something until changes are made

A. Philip Randolph

A. Philip Randolph was one of the leaders of the civil rights **movement**. In 1925, he had set up a labor union (a group that protects workers' rights) called the Brotherhood of Sleeping Car Porters. This was the first labor union for black workers.

Praying for Freedom

In 1957, Randolph organized a march to demand civil rights for black people. It was called the Prayer Pilgrimage for Freedom. Twenty-five thousand protesters met in Washington, D.C. It was the first large organized protest for civil rights.

◄ *People marched to Washington because it is the **capital** of the United States.*

> "Freedom is never given; it is won."
>
> A. Philip Randolph

movement: a group of people working together for a cause

13

For Jobs and Freedom

March on Washington

On Wednesday, August 28, 1963, A. Philip Randolph led another march on the capital. It was called the March on Washington for Jobs and Freedom. The march became one of the biggest **demonstrations** in the history of the United States.

By the Thousands

Organizers expected 100,000 people to gather in Washington for the march. Instead, about 250,000 protesters showed up! Most were African Americans. About 60,000 white people also marched that day, however.

◄ *No one expected so many protesters to march on Washington that day.*

"One thing that was remarkable about the day ... it was ... a mixed white and black crowd and everybody was friendly. There was really a good feeling in the air."

Robert Romer, a white teacher who attended the march

 demonstrations: public meetings or marches to protest something

Planning the Protest

A civil rights leader named Bayard Rustin organized the march. He had just two months to put together the biggest demonstration the world had ever seen. Rustin and his team carefully planned every detail so the protest would be orderly, peaceful, and safe.

▲ *Bayard Rustin (left) and his team worked hard to spread the word about the march.*

The Rules

The government and many people who lived in Washington were afraid that the crowd would turn **violent** and destroy the city. The government ruled that the march had to take place on a weekday. That way, fewer people would attend. Protesters were also told they had to arrive in the morning and leave before dark.

◀ *This building in Harlem, New York, was the headquarters for the march.*

City officials in Washington prepared for the worst. Thousands of police officers and soldiers were called in to protect the city. Hospitals got ready to treat large numbers of patients. Stores moved their goods out of town so they would not be stolen. People stayed home from work that day to be safe.

violent: using force to hurt or damage someone or something

Getting There

Local civil rights groups organized over 2,000 "freedom buses" and 30 "freedom trains" to get people to Washington. Many people traveled across the country from cities such as Boston, Milwaukee, Birmingham, St. Louis, and Little Rock.

▲ *Most protesters took hot, crowded bus rides that lasted for days. These marchers lined up early in the morning to board buses from New York.*

Brave Journey

Some people tried to keep protesters from getting on the "freedom buses." They sprayed water at the marchers and blocked their way with snarling dogs. People swore and shouted and threw things as the buses passed by. The protesters were determined to make it to the **historic** march, however.

"As the sun came up you see the whole freeway. All lanes completely jammed with buses. That's the moment we knew this march would be a big success."

Bruce Hartford, a student who came by bus to the march

historic: famous or important in history

Ready to Go

The march was set to begin at 11:30 a.m. on August 28. Buses and cars packed with people filled the streets of the city. Protesters gathered by the thousands at the Washington **Monument**. Most were dressed in their finest clothes for the important event.

▲ *The leaders of the march were running late, so they joined the middle of the crowd and posed for photos.*

Running Late

Randolph, Rustin, and other leaders of the march were running late that day. They were busy discussing the protest with members of the government. Much to their surprise, the eager crowd began to march without them!

"My God, they're going! We're supposed to be leading them!"

Bayard Rustin

monument: a statue or building made to honor someone important

Side by Side

Protesters waved signs demanding equal rights as they marched down the road. Black people walked side by side with white people. Many held hands to show they were **united**. Everyone used the same water fountains and restrooms that day.

▼ *Black people marched with white people shoulder to shoulder that day.*

All Together

Many different people took part in the March on Washington. Some were very poor. Others were rich and famous. Stars such as baseball player Jackie Robinson, singer Lena Horne, and actors Sidney Poitier and Marlon Brando took part in the historic march.

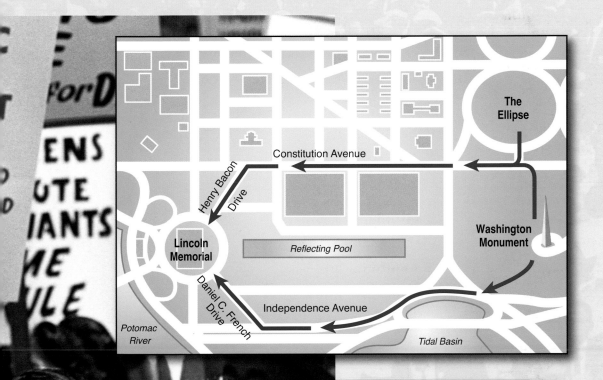

The Ellipse

Constitution Avenue

Henry Bacon Drive

Washington Monument

Lincoln Memorial

Reflecting Pool

Daniel C. French Drive

Independence Avenue

Potomac River

Tidal Basin

Some African Americans did not support the March on Washington. Malcolm X was a minister and civil rights leader. He did not think that black leaders should let white people take part in the march, which he called a "circus."

MARCH ON WASHINGTON FOR JOBS & FREEDOM WED. AUG. 28

united: joined together for a common goal

Lincoln Memorial

The march ended about a mile (1.6 km) away at the Lincoln Memorial. The Lincoln Memorial is a large monument built to honor Abraham Lincoln. President Lincoln had signed the Emancipation Proclamation in 1863. It freed the slaves in Confederate states during the American Civil War.

▼ *Civil rights leaders including Martin Luther King, Jr. (front row, second from right), A. Philip Randolph (front row, center) and John Lewis (back row, third from left) stand in front of the statue of Abraham Lincoln.*

100 Years Later

In 1865, the Thirteenth Amendment to the U.S. Constitution was passed outlawing slavery everywhere in the United States. Nearly 100 years later, African Americans' fight for **equality** continued at Lincoln's monument.

African Americans were used as slaves for hundreds of years. They worked long hours doing hard jobs with no pay. They did not have the freedom to make their own choices.

equality: being equal, having the same rights and freedom

MARCH ON WASHINGTON
FOR
JOBS & FREEDOM
AUGUST 28, 1963

On the Steps

The program began with the singing of the national anthem. A leader of the Catholic Church welcomed the marchers with a prayer. Then a number of people gave **passionate** speeches. They stood on the steps of the Lincoln Memorial and spoke to the huge crowd below.

▶ *A. Philip Randolph and other leaders shared their important message with the world that day.*

A Shared Vision

The speakers were leaders of different civil rights groups and churches. They had different races, religions, and points of view. They all voiced the need for change in America.

▼ *Josephine Baker said to the crowd: "I am glad that in my home this day has come to pass ... The world is behind you."*

MARCH ON **WASHINGTON** FOR **JOBS** & **FREEDOM** WED. AUG. 28

Jazz singer Josephine Baker was the only woman who gave a speech at the march. She praised the work of Rosa Parks and other women freedom fighters.

 passionate: having strong feelings about something

John Lewis

John Lewis gave one of the most powerful speeches of the day. Lewis was the head of a large **organization** of student protesters. His speech attacked the government for allowing black people in the South to be beaten by police and arrested without cause.

▼ *John Lewis was only 23 years old when he spoke to the world that day.*

James Farmer

James Farmer was the leader of a group that used peaceful ways to fight for equal rights for black people. Farmer was supposed to give a speech at the march, but he was in jail for protesting in Louisiana. Another civil rights worker read Farmer's speech at the march.

"We are tired of being beat by policemen. We are tired of seeing our people locked up in jail … We want our freedom and we want it now."

Excerpt from John Lewis's speech at the march

organization: a group of people working together

29

Protest Songs

Between speeches, popular folk singers entertained the crowd. They performed protest songs of all kinds. The marchers sang along. They clapped their hands.

▼ *Folk singers Joan Baez and Bob Dylan performed at the March on Washington.*

Singing for Change

Joan Baez sang protest songs called "We Shall Overcome" and "Oh, Freedom." Bob Dylan sang about the murder of a black civil rights protester named Medgar Evers. Mahalia Jackson wowed the crowd with the gospel song "How I Got Over."

"We Shall Overcome" became an **anthem** for the civil rights movement. People held hands and sang the song at the end of demonstrations and meetings. The song gave many protesters the hope and strength to keep fighting.

anthem: an uplifting song associated with a group or cause

Martin Luther King, Jr.

Martin Luther King, Jr. gave the final speech of the day. King was a Baptist minister and a powerful speaker. He was also a great leader of African Americans and their fight for freedom.

▼ *King's most famous speech is the one he gave at the March on Washington.*

King and Country

King believed in peaceful protest. He led thousands of blacks in the 1955 Montgomery Bus Boycott. King spoke at the 1957 Prayer Pilgrimage, where he **urged** the government to give African Americans the right to vote.

▲ *King took part in many peaceful demonstrations, such as this one in 1960.*

"Let's win at Washington."

Excerpt from March on Washington program

urged: tried hard to convince someone to do something

The King's Speech

Martin Luther King, Jr. spoke passionately about the need for equal rights. He talked about slavery and the chains of **discrimination** that still held African Americans. He urged blacks and whites to take action together to make changes.

I Have a Dream

King also talked about his hopes and faith for the future. Throughout his speech, he repeated the words for which he would be best remembered: "I have a dream." Then King described a world without segregation, where people are judged by their actions and not their skin color.

▼ *King's 19-minute speech helped change the course of history.*

"I have a dream that my four little children will one day live in a nation where they will not be judged by the color of their skin, but by the content of their character."

Martin Luther King, Jr.

discrimination: unfair treatment due to someone's race, sex, or age

The Demands

After King's speech, Randolph and Rustin read a list of demands for basic civil rights. The leaders wanted good jobs and homes for all Americans. They asked to share public buildings and go to good schools together. They also demanded that blacks be given the right to vote.

The Pledge

Then Randolph and Rustin asked the crowd to pledge, or promise, to keep fighting. The marchers swore together to take action for civil rights. The strong voices of 250,000 people were heard loud and clear that day.

◀ *Bayard Rustin urged the marchers to keep fighting for civil rights.*

"What counted most at the Lincoln Memorial was not the speeches ... but the pledge of a quarter million Americans, black and white, to carry the civil rights **revolution** into the streets."

Bayard Rustin

revolution: a major change in ways of thinking and behaving

We Shall Overcome

People held hands as the demonstration came to an end. The marchers prayed together. Then they raised their voices as one and sang "We Shall Overcome." By 4:20 p.m., the march was over.

▼ *Protesters joined hands and sang and prayed together.*

Back to the Buses

People slowly made their way back to the buses. Some sang or laughed together as they walked. Others talked with new hope about the future. Most had joy in their hearts and a new bounce in their step.

▲ *This picture shows crowds of people filling Union Station in Washington as they head home after the march.*

"We ... see the Washington March as wrapping up the dreams, hopes, **ambitions**, tears, and prayers of millions who have lived for this day."

Excerpt from the March on Washington program

 ambitions: strong desires to achieve something

MARCH ON WASHINGTON
FOR
JOBS & FREEDOM
AUGUST 28, 1963

Good News

Hundreds of reporters covered the events of the day. Camera crews **broadcasted** the march, speeches, and songs live around the world. Viewers were amazed that the huge demonstration was so orderly and peaceful. They found new respect for the civil rights movement.

Civil Rights King

Martin Luther King, Jr. became a hero. *Time* magazine named him "Man of the Year" for 1963. A year later, King was given the Nobel Peace Prize. This award is given each year to a person or organization that has worked hard to achieve peace.

◀ *This picture shows an NBC camera crew filming the March on Washington. Millions of Americans watched the historic march live on TV.*

NEW YORK CHANNEL **4**

"The world saw for itself the best side of the civil rights movement."

Excerpt from a British government report on the march

broadcasted: sent out a radio or television program

Marching On

The success of the march gave many protesters the hope and courage to carry on. It also showed the government that both black and white Americans wanted change. After the march, King, Randolph, and other civil rights leaders met with President Kennedy to discuss new laws.

▼ *President Kennedy (fourth from right) meets with civil rights leaders in 1963.*

Class Acts

One year later, the Civil Rights Act of 1964 was passed. The law made discrimination of any kind **illegal** in the United States. It also ended segregation in schools, jobs, and public spaces. A year after that, the Voting Rights Act of 1965 was passed. The new law gave African Americans the right to vote.

"I believe in an America that is on the march ... an America that is moving, doing, working, trying—a strong America in a world of peace."

President John F. Kennedy

illegal: against the law

Looking Back

Today, people **commemorate** the March on Washington for Jobs and Freedom. Many take part in peaceful marches to the Lincoln Memorial to remember the 1963 march and to protest other causes. Americans honor Martin Luther King, Jr. with a national holiday each January.

▶ *Half a million people came to the Lincoln Memorial to celebrate the 20th anniversary of the March on Washington.*

Timeline

1955 Rosa Parks' protest starts Montgomery Bus Boycott

1957 Prayer Pilgrimage for Freedom

1960 Four black students take part in first "sit-in," in Greensboro, North Carolina

1963 March on Washington for Jobs and Freedom

1964 Civil Rights Act; Martin Luther King, Jr. awarded Nobel Peace Prize

1965 Voting Rights Act

Looking Ahead

In 2011, a monument to King, the Martin Luther King, Jr. Memorial, opened in Washington D.C. In 2013, people around the world will celebrate the 50th anniversary of the March on Washington. They will honor King and the other brave civil rights workers who fought so hard for equality.

"Change has never been simple ... Change depends on persistence. Change requires determination."

U.S. President Barack Obama, speaking at the dedication of King's memorial

commemorate: to remember and respect someone or something

Learning More

Books

DK Biography: Martin Luther King, Jr.
by Amy Pastan
(DK Publishing, Inc., 2004)

Landmark Events in American History: The 1963 Civil Rights March
by Scott Ingram
(World Almanac Library, 2004)

Primary Source Readers: Civil Rights Movement
by Wendy Conklin
(Teacher Created Materials Publishing, 2008)

The March on Washington
by James Haskins
(Just Us Books, 2004)

Websites

www.nationalarchives.gov.uk/education/heroesvillains/g6/
The National Archives: Martin Luther King and the Civil Rights Movement

www.pbs.org/wgbh/amex/eyesontheprize/story/08_washington.html
Eyes on the Prize: America's Civil Rights Movement

http://mlk-kpp01.stanford.edu/
The Martin Luther King, Jr. Research and Education Institute

DVDs

Eyes on the Prize: America's Civil Rights Years 1954–1965
A PBS documentary series about the civil rights movement

Glossary

ambitions Strong desires to achieve something

anthem An uplifting song associated with a group or cause

boycott A refusal to buy or use something until changes are made

broadcasted Sent out a radio or television program

capital The city where the government of a country is located

civil rights The rights given to people by their government

commemorate To remember and respect someone or something

demonstrations Public meetings or marches to protest something

discrimination Unfair treatment due to someone's race, sex, or age

equality Being equal, having the same rights and freedom

historic Famous or important in history

illegal Against the law

monument A statue or building made to honor someone important

movement A group of people working together for a cause

organization A group of people working together

passionate Having strong feelings about something

protests Actions to show that people disagree with something

revolution A major change in ways of thinking and behaving

segregation The separation of one group of people from another

united Joined together for a common goal

urged Tried hard to convince someone to do something

violent Using force to hurt or damage someone or something

Index

Entries in **bold** refer to pictures